DINOSAUR FACT DIG

EDMONTOSAURUS
AND OTHER DUCKBILLED DINOSAURS
THE NEED-TO-KNOW FACTS

BY
REBECCA RISSMAN

Consultant: Mathew J. Wedel, PhD
Associate Professor
Western University of Health Services

CAPSTONE PRESS
a capstone imprint

A+ Books are published by Capstone Press,
1710 Roe Crest Drive, North Mankato, Minnesota 56003
www.mycapstone.com

Library of Congress Cataloging-in-Publication Data
Names: Rissman, Rebecca, author.
Title: Edmontosaurus and other duckbilled dinosaurs : the need-to-know facts
/ by Rebecca Rissman.
Description: North Mankato, Minnesota : Capstone Press, [2017] | Series: A+
books. Dinosaur fact dig | Audience: Ages 6–8 | Audience: K to grade 3 | Includes
bibliographical references and index.
Identifiers: LCCN 2015048109| ISBN 9781515726982 (library binding) | ISBN
9781515727026 (pbk.) | ISBN 9781515727064 (ebook (pdf))
Subjects: LCSH: Edmontosaurus—Juvenile literature. | Dinosaurs—Juvenile literature.
Classification: LCC QE862.O65 R57 2017 | DDC 567.914—dc23
LC record available at http://lccn.loc.gov/2015048109

EDITORIAL CREDITS:

Michelle Hasselius, editor; Kazuko Collins, designer; Wanda Winch, media researcher;
Gene Bentdahl, production specialist

IMAGE CREDITS: All images by Jon Hughes except: MapArt (maps), Shutterstock: Elena
Elisseeva, green gingko leaf, Jiang Hongyan, yellow gingko leaf, Taigi, paper background

Printed in China.
022016   007586

**NOTE TO PARENTS, TEACHERS,
AND LIBRARIANS:**
This Dinosaur Fact Dig book uses
full-color images and a nonfiction
format to introduce the concept of
duckbilled dinosaurs. *Edmontosaurus
and Other Duckbilled Dinosaurs* is
designed to be read aloud to a pre-reader
or to be read independently by an early
reader. Images help listeners and early
readers understand the text and concepts
discussed. The book encourages further
learning by including the following sections:
Table of Contents, Glossary, Critical Thinking
Using the Common Core, Read More,
Internet Sites, and Index. Early readers may
need assistance using these features.

TABLE OF CONTENTS

Edmontosaurus might have been a dinosaur, but it had a lot in common with today's ducks. Edmontosaurus had a broad, flat bill, similar to a duck's beak. The dinosaur also swam in water.

Edmontosaurus and other duckbilled dinosaurs lived between 85 and 65 million years ago. All dinosaurs in this group had ducklike beaks. Some also had crests on top of their heads. Find out more about Edmontosaurus and other duckbilled dinosaurs, such as Lambeosaurus, Maiasaura, and Lophorhothon.

CHARONOSAURUS

PRONOUNCED: shar-OWN-o-SAWR-us

NAME MEANING: Charon's lizard; named after a Greek mythical figure

TIME PERIOD LIVED: Late Cretaceous Period

LENGTH: 32 feet (10 meters)

WEIGHT: 5.5 tons (5 metric tons)

TYPE OF EATER: herbivore

PHYSICAL FEATURES: sturdy tail; thick legs; large bony crest on its head

CHARONOSAURUS blew through its crest to call to other dinosaurs. It probably sounded like a loud trumpet.

Charonosaurus lived in the forests of what is now China.

N
W E
S

■

where this dinosaur lived

CHARONOSAURUS walked on four legs. It could also stand up on its back legs to reach tall branches.

Scientists think dinosaurs like **CHARONOSAURUS** had hipbones that looked similar to a bird's hipbones.

CORYTHOSAURUS

PRONOUNCED: KOR-ith-o-SAWR-us

NAME MEANING: helmet lizard

TIME PERIOD LIVED: Late Cretaceous Period

LENGTH: 26 feet (8 m)

WEIGHT: 3 tons (2.7 metric tons)

TYPE OF EATER: herbivore

PHYSICAL FEATURES: large teeth; thick legs; large crest on its head

CORYTHOSAURUS probably grazed on ferns and other low-growing plants.

Corythosaurus lived in the forests and swamps of what are now Canada and the United States.

N
W E
S

■ where this dinosaur lived

Scientists thought **CORYTHOSAURUS'** crest looked like the helmets worn by ancient Greek soldiers.

Scientists discovered a **CORYTHOSAURUS** fossil that showed what the dinosaur's leathery skin looked like.

EDMONTOSAURUS

PRONOUNCED: ed-MON-toe-SAWR-us

NAME MEANING: royal reptile from Edmonton; named after the Edmonton rock formation, where its fossils were found

TIME PERIOD LIVED: Late Cretaceous Period

LENGTH: 30 feet (9 m)

WEIGHT: 3.9 tons (3.5 metric tons)

TYPE OF EATER: herbivore

PHYSICAL FEATURES: wide beak; boneless crest on top of its head

EDMONTOSAURUS had up to 2,000 teeth. They locked together to grind up food.

EDMONTOSAURUS ate conifers. It probably also grazed on low plants.

Edmontosaurus lived in the forests and swamps of what are now Canada and the United States.

where this dinosaur lived

N
W E
S

Tyrannosaurus rex was one of **EDMONTOSAURUS'** main predators.

HADROSAURUS

PRONOUNCED: HAD-ro-SAWR-us

NAME MEANING: sturdy lizard

TIME PERIOD LIVED: Late Cretaceous Period

LENGTH: 23 feet (7 m)

WEIGHT: 2.2 tons (2 metric tons)

TYPE OF EATER: herbivore

PHYSICAL FEATURES: strong legs; short arms; wide beak

HADROSAURUS bones were found in 1858. It was the first dinosaur discovered in North America.

Hadrosaurus lived in the forests and swamps of what is now the United States.

N
W E
S

where this dinosaur lived

HADROSAURUS was the first dinosaur to have its skeleton put on display.

HADROSAURUS lived in big herds, similar to other dinosaurs in this group.

KRITOSAURUS

PRONOUNCED: KRIT-o-SAWR-us

NAME MEANING: separated lizard

TIME PERIOD LIVED: Late Cretaceous Period

LENGTH: 26 feet (8 m)

WEIGHT: 3.3 tons (3 metric tons)

TYPE OF EATER: herbivore

PHYSICAL FEATURES: long legs and tail; short arms; small crest

KRITOSAURUS got its name because its cheekbones did not fit together well when it was first discovered.

Kritosaurus lived in the forests and swamps of what is now the southern United States.

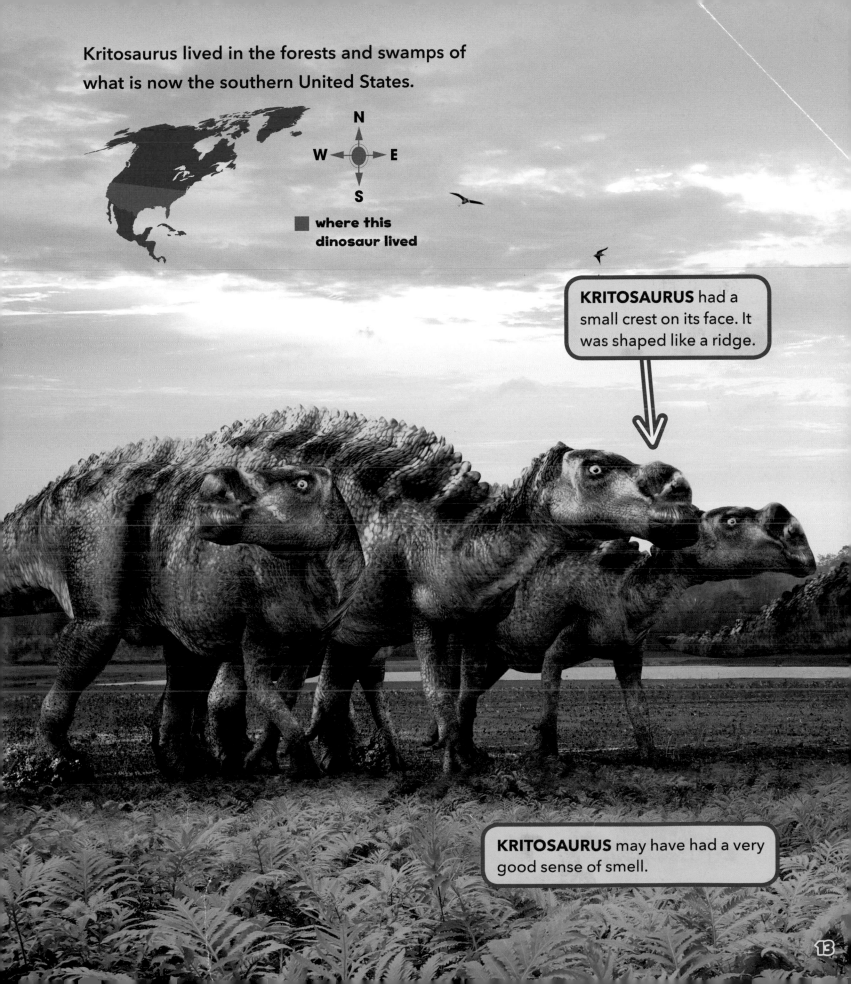

N
W E
S

■ where this dinosaur lived

KRITOSAURUS had a small crest on its face. It was shaped like a ridge.

KRITOSAURUS may have had a very good sense of smell.

LAMBEOSAURUS

PRONOUNCED: lam-BEE-o-SAWR-us

NAME MEANING: Lambe's lizard; named after Lawrence Lambe, a famous paleontologist

TIME PERIOD LIVED: Late Cretaceous Period

LENGTH: 29 feet (9 m)

WEIGHT: 2.6 tons (2.4 metric tons)

TYPE OF EATER: herbivore

PHYSICAL FEATURES: strong beak; large mitten-shaped crest on its head

LAMBEOSAURUS could probably hear very well.

LAMBEOSAURUS had a strong beak with many teeth to eat tough plants.

Lambeosaurus lived in the forests and swamps of what are now Canada, Mexico, and the United States.

■ where this dinosaur lived

N
W ◆ E
S

Scientists have had many ideas about how **LAMBEOSAURUS** used its crest. One was that the dinosaur used it as a snorkel to swim underwater.

LOPHORHOTHON

PRONOUNCED: LOF-or-HOH-thon

NAME MEANING: crested nose

TIME PERIOD LIVED: Late Cretaceous Period

LENGTH: 15 feet (4.5 m)

WEIGHT: 2 tons (1.8 metric tons)

TYPE OF EATER: herbivore

PHYSICAL FEATURES: short arms; strong legs; small crest over its eyes

LOPHORHOTHON may have chewed tough plants for a long time before swallowing, like cows do today.

Lophorhothon lived in the forests of what is now the United States.

N
W E
S

where this dinosaur lived

LOPHORHOTHON had a very thick, strong tail.

The first **LOPHORHOTHON** fossils were discovered in Alabama in 1940.

MAIASAURA

PRONOUNCED: MY-a-SAWR-uh

NAME MEANING: good mother lizard

TIME PERIOD LIVED: Late Cretaceous Period

LENGTH: 23 feet (7 m)

WEIGHT: 2.8 tons (2.5 metric tons)

TYPE OF EATER: herbivore

PHYSICAL FEATURES: tail used for balance; narrow beak; small crests over its eyes

Scientists have discovered **MAIASAURA** nests. They have found fossils of unhatched eggs, babies, and adults inside the nests.

Maiasaura lived in the forests of what is now the United States.

where this dinosaur lived

It took about seven or eight years for **MAIASAURA** to reach full size.

Fossils show that **MAIASAURA** babies could not walk right away. They needed to be cared for by adults.

OLOROTITAN

PRONOUNCED: oh-LAW-ro-TYE-tan

NAME MEANING: giant swan

TIME PERIOD LIVED: Late Cretaceous Period

LENGTH: 26 feet (8 m)

WEIGHT: 3.4 tons (3.1 metric tons)

TYPE OF EATER: herbivore

PHYSICAL FEATURES: stiff tail; long neck; fan-shaped crest on its head

OLOROTITAN probably used its long neck to bite leaves from tall trees.

Olorotitan lived in the forests of what is now Russia.

where this dinosaur lived

N
W E
S

OLOROTITAN could have used its crest to scare away other dinosaurs, similar to what frilled lizards do today.

Another theory is dinosaurs like **OLOROTITAN** may have used their crests to identify one another.

PARASAUROLOPHUS

PRONOUNCED: PAR-uh-SAWR-oh-LOH-fus

NAME MEANING: like Saurolophus; Saurolophus was another duckbilled dinosaur with a smaller crest

TIME PERIOD LIVED: Late Cretaceous Period

LENGTH: 25 feet (7.5 m)

WEIGHT: 2.9 tons (2.6 metric tons)

TYPE OF EATER: herbivore

PHYSICAL FEATURES: beak; long crest on its head; strong legs

PARASAUROLOPHUS is one of the most famous duckbilled dinosaurs because of its unique crest.

Parasaurolophus lived in the forests of what is now the United States and Canada.

N
W E
S

where this
dinosaur
lived

PARASAUROLOPHUS
was discovered in 1922 by paleontologist William Parks. The dinosaur Parksosaurus was named in honor of Parks.

At first scientists thought **PARASAUROLOPHUS** used its crest to fight other dinosaurs. Today few scientists think this theory is true.

SAUROLOPHUS

PRONOUNCED: SAWR-oh-LOH-fus

NAME MEANING: ridged lizard

TIME PERIOD LIVED: Late Cretaceous Period

LENGTH: 27 feet (8.2 m)

WEIGHT: 3.3 tons (3 metric tons)

TYPE OF EATER: herbivore

PHYSICAL FEATURES: strong legs; thick tail; spike-shaped crest on its head

SAUROLOPHUS could run and walk on its back legs. This may have helped the dinosaur escape from predators.

Saurolophus lived in the forests and swamps of what are now Canada and Mongolia.

N
W ←●→ E
S

■ where this dinosaur lived

Paleontologist Barnum Brown named **SAUROLOPHUS**. Brown was a famous fossil hunter who discovered the first Tyrannosaurus rex.

SAUROLOPHUS may have had a brightly colored crest. This could have helped it stand out to other dinosaurs.

SHANTUNGOSAURUS

PRONOUNCED: SHAN-tung-uh-SAWR-us

NAME MEANING: Shandong lizard; fossils were first discovered in the Shandong, China

TIME PERIOD LIVED: Late Cretaceous Period

LENGTH: 50 feet (15 m)

WEIGHT: 14.3 tons (13 metric tons)

TYPE OF EATER: herbivore

PHYSICAL FEATURES: wide beak; thick legs; strong arms

SHANTUNGOSAURUS had more than 1,000 teeth.

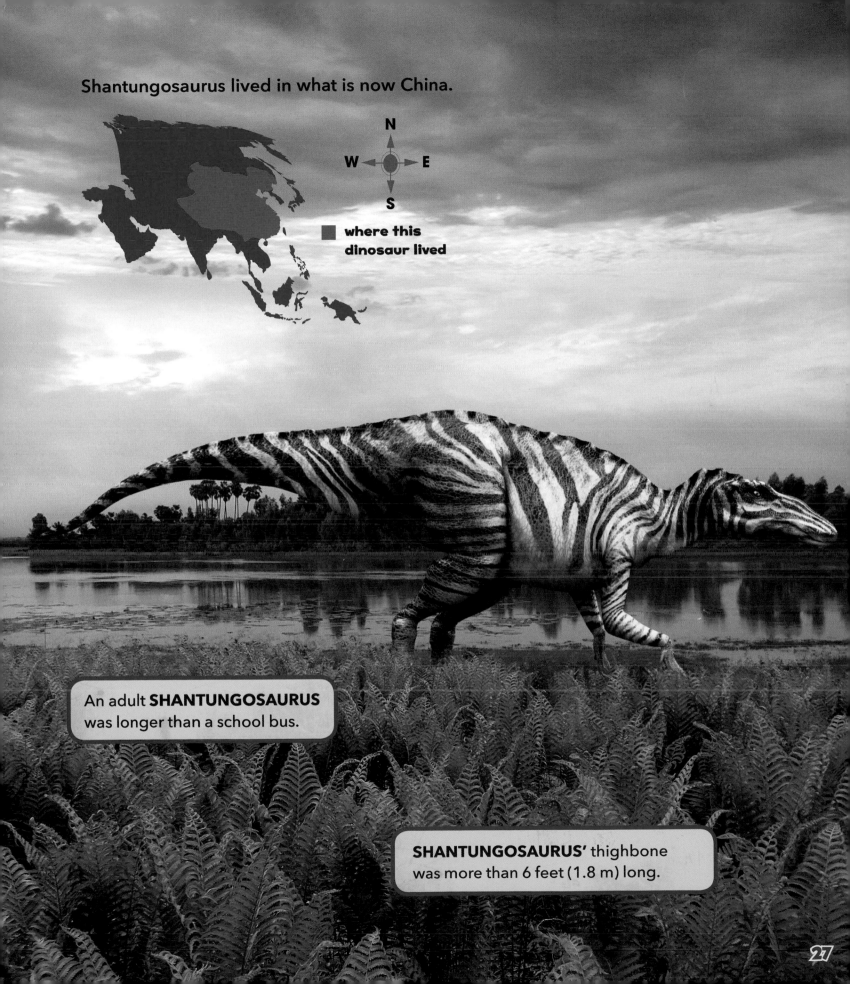

Shantungosaurus lived in what is now China.

N
W ← → E
S

where this
dinosaur lived

An adult **SHANTUNGOSAURUS**
was longer than a school bus.

SHANTUNGOSAURUS' thighbone
was more than 6 feet (1.8 m) long.

TSINTAOSAURUS

PRONOUNCED: SIN-tow-SAWR-us

NAME MEANING: Tsingtao lizard; fossils were first discovered in Tsingtao, China

TIME PERIOD LIVED: Late Cretaceous Period

LENGTH: 27 feet (8.2 m)

WEIGHT: 2.8 tons (2.5 metric tons)

TYPE OF EATER: herbivore

PHYSICAL FEATURES: strong legs; thick tail; beak; fan-shaped crest on top of its head

TSINTAOSAURUS grew new teeth after its old teeth wore down.

Tsintaosaurus lived in what is now China.

N
W E
S

where this
dinosaur lived

TSINTAOSAURUS had many
flat teeth to chew through
tough plants.

For a long time, scientists thought
TSINTAOSAURUS' crest looked like a unicorn's
horn. Newly discovered fossils show that its crest
was shaped like a fan, similar to the crests of
Corythosaurus and Olorotitan.

GLOSSARY

ANCIENT (AYN-shunt)—from a long time ago

BEAK (BEEK)—the hard part of a bird's mouth; some dinosaurs had beaks

CONIFER (KON-uh-fur)—a tree with cones and narrow leaves called needles

CREST (KREST)—a flat plate of bone

CRETACEOUS PERIOD (krah-TAY-shus PIHR-ee-uhd)—the third period of the Mesozoic Era; the Cretaceous Period was from 145 to 65 million years ago

FERN (FUHRN)—a plant with long, thin leaves called fronds

FOSSIL (FOSS-uhl)—the remains of an animal or plant from millions of years ago that have turned to rock

FRILLED LIZARD (FRILD LIZ-urhd)—a large lizard with a broad frill on each side of its neck; frilled lizards live in Australia

GRAZE (GRAYZ)—to eat grass and other plants growing in fields

HERBIVORE (HUR-buh-vor)—an animal that eats only plants

HERD (HURD)—a large group of animals that lives or travels together

IDENTIFY (eye-DEN-tuh-fye)—to tell what something is or who someone is

PALEONTOLOGIST (pale-ee-uhn-TOL-uh-jist)—a scientist who studies fossils

PREDATOR (PRED-uh-tur)—an animal that hunts other animals for food

PRONOUNCE (proh-NOUNSS)—to say a word in a certain way

SNORKEL (SNOR-kuhl)—a tube used to breathe through when swimming underwater

THEORY (THEE-ur-ee)—an idea that explains something that is unknown

TRUMPET (TRUHM-pit)—an instrument with a long, looped tube that ends in a funnel shape, with three valves used to change the tones

CRITICAL THINKING USING THE COMMON CORE

1. Tyrannosaurus rex was one of Edmontosaurus' main predators. What is a predator? (Craft and Structure)

2. What was the name of the first dinosaur discovered in North America? (Key Ideas and Details)

3. Describe two ways Olorotitan could have used its crest. (Key Ideas and Details)

READ MORE

Riehecky, Janet. *Show Me Dinosaurs: My First Picture Encyclopedia.* My First Picture Encyclopedias. North Mankato, Minn.: Capstone Press, 2013.

Rockwood, Leigh. *Hadrosaurus.* Dinosaurs Ruled! New York: PowerKids Press, 2012.

Zeiger, Jennifer. *Maiasaura.* Dinosaurs. Ann Arbor, Mich.: Cherry Lake Publishing, 2014.

INTERNET SITES

FactHound offers a safe, fun way to find Internet sites related to this book. All of the sites on FactHound have been researched by our staff.

Here's all you do:

Visit *www.facthound.com*

Type in this code: 9781515726982

Check out projects, games and lots more at
www.capstonekids.com

INDEX